The Walnut Tree

Tim Slade is a Tasmanian poet. His poems have received praise in the Margaret Reid International Poetry Prize, the Janice Bostock Haiku Award, the Australian Cricket Poetry Prize and the Henry Lawson Festival Award.

Tim's poems have been published widely, including in *The Weekend Australian, The Koori Mail, Australian Poetry Anthology, Growing Up Disabled In Australia* and *Cordite Poetry Review.*

In the years 2013 – 2021, Tim has contributed twenty-five articles for *Tasmanian Times* (online), investigating the recurring health risk from heavy metals in the drinking water at Pioneer. Tim has volunteered as an advocate for the community, and he has worked to reform the policies and practices affecting drinking water in Tasmania.

Born in 1976, Tim was raised in Hobart's Risdon Cove, in the industrial suburb of Lutana. He graduated from UTAS as a school teacher, but his career was curtailed early by chronic auto-immune illnesses.

In 2009 Tim moved to the tiny town of Pioneer, near the Blue Tier, in Tasmania's north-east. Over the span of a decade, from his tin-miner's cottage, Tim wrote the poems for his debut collection, *The Walnut Tree.*

The Walnut Tree

Tim Slade

First published in 2021 by Bright South (Tasmania, Australia)
www.brightsouth.com.au

© Tim Slade, 2021
www.tim-slade.jimdosite.com

© Cover Image: Robert McDonald, 'A Quiet Place'
www.vickimdkidd.wixsite.com/arveartgallery

Copyright is retained by the author. Except for the purpose of fair dealing, no part of this publication may be reproduced, stored in a retrieval system, or transmitted in any form, by any means, without prior permission from the publisher.

Tim Slade
The Walnut Tree
ISBN 978-0-6481798-3-2 Paperback
ISBN 978-0-6481798-4-9 EBook
1. Australian Poetry – 21st Century. I. Title.

Contents

I.

The Walnut Tree	1
Supermoon	3
Thylacine	4
Torana	5
The Green Religion	6
On the Day Les Murray Died	7
The Wand of the Sea	9
The Funeral	11
A Life Jacket is Found at Salamanca	12
Georgia	13
Teacup of the Rose	14
The Wave	15
Our Cricket Moon	16
Life Buoy Café	17

II.

Untitled	21
A Yorta Yorta Man	22
Factory at Risdon Cove	24
A Terra Nullius Election	25
The Wrecking Yard	26
The Clock-Maker of Launceston	27
Tiger Snake	29
A Body's Civil War	31
Cricket is Proof of Eternity	33
The Memory of a Cyclone	35
A Bit of Healthy Conversation	36
The Encyclopedias of Van Diemen's Land	37
Van Diemen's Land	39
Fog	40
The Jockey-Wheel of Faith	41

Endeavour at the Opera House	42
Mermaid	44
Detours	46

III.

A Wisdom of Wombats	49
How to Read a Poem	50
Auden's Web	53
Penny-Farthing	54
Blue Derby	55
Postie	57
A Lotus of Lawyers	58
Skeet, the Woodman	60
The Gum Leaf Player	61
Unreasonable Happiness	63
Child and Grandfather	64
The Future Library	66
The Ant	67

Acknowledgements
Thank you

When he held a flower for the first time,
he smelled it without thinking and fell asleep.
From day one, he was a fighter.

Andy Jackson
'Dalton'.

THE WALNUT TREE

'I hope I dream about the trees all night.'
George Mackay Brown, 'Trees'.

Winter –
fog envelops
the walnut tree.

Flannelette sheets, damp
along the branches
of a Hills Hoist.

Beyond the grey paling fence:
kunanyi, snow-capped.
Our neighbour,

Reg smiles – a master carpenter's
horn-rimmed spectacles, cardigan
scent of Huon pine;

and Edna – her head bowed
towards me, as though reading –
she turns an early page...

It is my eighth birthday.
I sit astride a new Mustang,
my mother's golden gift

of innocent transportation.
The shortest day of the year
upon the icy breath of Hobart.

She who frames the memory,
my grandmother, Margaret –
'Smi-le!... Ti-mmy!...'

I ring the bell of my bicycle;
her Instamatic's shutter opens:
the timing of love.

I begin to know
the *what will be*
of this photograph...

Today, her writing desk,
chest of drawers, bookshelf –
but I can never return.

A need to have what she felt
more deeply understood:
to take root –

my whole life
before me, beneath
the walnut tree...

SUPERMOON

Branxholm, Tasmania – 2020.

For Chris and Clare.

At the biggest moon I have ever seen,
I remember the words of a young friend
who an hour or two earlier, roadside,
told me that his chemo will never end:

he was being factual; and with no hint
of drama, neither comedy nor tragedy.
I was having trouble hearing him
over the rolling trucks. He is ready

like no man I have ever seen be.
Ready. As one who returns from a walk
with his beloved, along the quiet track
through bush and a ghostly farm where talk

does not need to be, and so to learn –
as the waning of the moon that will not return.

THYLACINE

*'As an invisible spirit of All-life
the clear water is all-clear forever.'*

Jim Everett (puralia meenamatta)
and Jonathan Kimberley, 'Water'.

You are looking without seeing.
Myth, cocoon of black stripes, pouch,
ungula prints of this rainforest's endling…
A blind jaw traps: encapsulates two million years.
Masked owl, white goshawk, is she the last?
Remember her, sun-sifted into freedom
at this sweet-tasting river of the Blue Tier.

In the golden pouch of night, is it a dream –
rope-tailed, curious – if downstream
a white man at the coming of the dawn
by the river, shivers in the All-life
of this mirror? In morning's sunroom
a butterfly: winged with light the all-seeing river,
mirror to a papier-mâché sun.

Note:
The word thylacine is from thylakos, the Greek word for pouch.

TORANA

Torana is an Aboriginal word, meaning: to fly.

The day of his funeral, Melbourne is a Dali timepiece.
I look about me, but nobody seems to have noticed
the Torana: it's a rare and shiny thing when an answer
falls out of the sky in the city. In the rear-view mirror

the turntable suburbs; and from open windows:
'I'm livin' in the seventies!... I'm livin' in the seventies!...'
The Torana turns on its fat wheels from Flinders,
snaps back on its line into Swanston, like a tram –

but with bounce... Melbourne's boom-box is just
a mirage: *'...I feel like a bar man... who can't drink a beer...'*
From the street, I peer inside the teal Torana – our eyes meet –
I am his witness. But who will believe we were here?

For Skyhooks – for Shirl – he revs the V8 of 1975 –
the handbrake is a stylus lowered to the sound –
a record of the suburbs, the Torana's rhythm tracks
to fly round the block – once more – *encore...*

Note:
'Livin' in the Seventies', Skyhooks.

THE GREEN RELIGION

Risdon Cove, Tasmania.

You swoop to kiss the manicured green
as if you'd just tamed an eagle...

Playing with faith, here's your torn
glove, a palm-sized *Bible of Golf;*
the wedges, irons, slammers, Sunday.

Still as a prayer the summoned shadow –
putter, prone. Your lucky Pinnacle.

In the lower zip-pocket, echidna coins –
an otherwise solitary train of males
through rough, along fairways, nose-to-tail,
evolved to seek the single soft-shelled egg
and the hole of *Monotremata*.

Perhaps religion is an animal's constellation
of flag positions, but here, beneath a raven-black
umbrella: proof-in-pencil of a hole in one.

Now the innocence of Spring's first tee-off
at dawn. Round an Amen dogleg

the headstone reads: *Life Member.*

ON THE DAY LES MURRAY DIED

In memory of Leslie Allan Murray, 17 October, 1938 – 29 April, 2019.

'Humans are flown, or fall; humans can't fly.'
Les Murray, 'To Fly In Just Your Suit'.

Early this day I am lifting my head
to the light. There is a need for firewood –
tomorrow and May before winter comes,
the shed yawns, as one who has early stood.

With another winter on the warpath,
the dream of wearing shorts forever, dims.
For gateposts – horse before the cart – the holes:
today I'll pick, shovel, palm for my sins.

For this new day, and since I first breathed air,
aware, in this sunshine, in this stillness –
which only an autumn day may create –
a perfection cannot be any less.

The cursive ground troubles me for a while,
but it is in the action of doing
I learn anew just how it may be done:
like a new poem, mending self's undoing.

Perhaps the spirit level may ordain
the gates to swing sweetly at my entry?
With these gates I'll be in Heaven. Tonight
I shall open a book of poetry.

I lie on my belly in the grass. Look:
the red-ripe orchard, the sweet thought of her;
the old, purple terminal bloom – vinca –
the Latin translation is: *To Conquer.*

I down tools; pat the cat; then it is time
to watch the TV News (the ABC)...
The giant of Australian poetry, Les
Murray died today, eighty years. I see

the Bard of Bunyah – 'Hmmph... I am my poems.
That is where you will find me.' He is dead.
Absolutely ordinary rainbow
of wool. Peacefully, he has died in bed.

It's a busy news night, and poetry's
a snowflake's chance in hell to right the debt,
misery and corruption – even now
beneath the stars at the death of the great poet.

And it doesn't. But Les Murray's poems live.
I'll shine a light upon his life in words,
be grateful each time I find his smile.
Pray this is the way he flew with the birds.

Note:
Les Murray, 'An Absolutely Ordinary Rainbow'.

THE WAND OF THE SEA

Dunalley, Tasmania.

My grandfather's smile
at the handsome shore's
crooked geology.

Dementia's goblet:
biceps of blue make face in the middle and
gulp!

Stranger –
to recognise
your loved one's voice.

Today,
those-days,
these-days…

Crayfish
in the wishing well.
Glittering, beyond

one thousand years'
mast of Huon pine –
girls and boys

time-dive
for the beautiful
wake…

Sea birds glide
upon the forgetful
breeze…

My grandfather
gathers
the pocket watch

of his birth –
memory,
and the wish –

behind
the wand
of the sea...

The ward and wend
of His wand is
black...

THE FUNERAL

For my grandfather, Brian (Mick) Wiggins.

A seagull buries beak into feathers to sleep...

Now is the time to anchor
our hearts. My grandfather sails
into unchartered waters. The church –

shiny shoes shuffle, and the logbook
turns back this old salt's pages
to the first of his life. Today,

nailed sternwards from the mast of a cray boat:
No Salesmen, Religious or Otherwise...
We would see him last at the funeral

for his wife, Margaret. Walking down the aisle
go I. Then starboard, towards an unknown
horizon. We are now at the mercy

of the current of the church...

A LIFE JACKET IS FOUND AT SALAMANCA

Includes words from Margaret Scott's poem, 'Southern Ocean'.

I blinded the shield,
and I blinded the night.

The power to see into strangeness
and live in the ocean's heart
to join in the universal dance,
and bear a gentle part.

A palm tells the fortune
of a heart split in two; shards
the palm reader is at pains

to explain. Two heart lines
in the palm of one hand. A heart:
two hearts; and none.

GEORGIA

For Corey, Melissa, Claire and Danah.

In memory of my baby niece,
6 April, 2003 – 1 May, 2003.

Gather (family, hands, past, present, future)...
Recall (birth, touch, face, voice, breath)...
Inter (stars, moon, dreams, body, earth)...
Eternal (love, light, water, air, memories)...
Visit (day, surrender, faith, photographs, night)...
Elegy (heartbeat, newborn, evanescence, hope, life)...

TEACUP OF THE ROSE

The rose is painted red. There is no other
teacup of the rose unbroken. I bring it to my mother.

She cries, for her mother's rose garden
once tended with love. When my mother sleeps, please pardon:

she is an orphan now. Her father, long of the sea, mute;
or could not say, 'I love you'. Cold hands shall not refute

the strike of a match. Her mother and father's ashes
this day scattered. Teacup of the rose; moist lashes.

Hobart's roses: Blossom Time, Happenstance; Alchemist, First Crush –
Moonlight, Awakening; New Dawn, Gold Blush –

Yellow Butterfly, Compassion; Quietness, Sea Breeze –
and the rose of her mother's name – Margaret. On her knees,

a shelf of mysteries thorny as any rose; and blood rows
of family photographs, framed. Petal conscious my mother knows

the perfume of cut roses in a vase, and the five pinnate leaves
of a secret – to be *under the rose*. A rose window weaves

a wheel of sunlight; beyond, the card of a mariner's
compass is called a rose. Navigating imagined silk, secateurs

cut the bush back hard at the last frost. A rosedrop of blood.
May this ward away the grief of the rose beetle. For rosebud.

My mother brings the teacup to her lips, a red rose
painted upon each cheek. It is my love for her, I suppose.

THE WAVE

After Clive James' epic poem, 'The River in the Sky'.

As time rolls in, the sure threat of each breath;
of the breath of the fact of one's own death.
When to be awoken from this Earth dream?
And as your next breath happens to be true,

might the breath of a poem awaken you –
of the breath of the fact of one's own death –
to this Earth dream?   A father: lost.   *The Flash
of Lightning*. I am reading the last page

of 'The River in the Sky', by Clive James;
a rogue wave rolling sudden to the shore,
the poem thunders, then it is gone once more.
I'm of daydream in one of the sunroom's

two chairs. Am I awake? Of breath, exiled:
my father. Earth's only moon. Poet as child.

Note:
The Flash of Lightning: Clive James' childhood alter ego –
'You would not have known, when this sinister avatar
caught and slipped your startled gaze, that his mask
and cape had been made by his mother.' Clive James,
Unreliable Memoirs.

OUR CRICKET MOON

For Bronwyn.

In memory of Alison Dewing and Stephen Hill.

Know the UFO... Playing a straight bat
to a flash of light and the spinning seam, in slow-motion
a father's son's eyes close... Beneath our cricket moon

he dreams of the planet-heavy universe:
Boon, Marsh, Jones, the Waugh twins, Border... The order
and their bearing upon play here on Earth.

The world of cricket – longitude and latitude –
we study catching co-ordinates, pray
for a *classic catch*, just as the girls are sighted

on the horizon. A girl named Gloria Kiss
fumbles a book of love poems; I catch
her library card, read the two-word poem...

>*KISS, Gloria.*

Last day at primary school – Save Our Souls –
the boys are shipwrecked around an upturned
blade of willow. Like a century of times before,

but this time every girl we have ever known
drifts out of sight. It feels like *forever*. Today,
safe at home within the white picket fence –

those boys are lost; and only eleven.

LIFE BUOY CAFÉ

I.

I read Sarah Day's poem, *Jetty*.

II.

Birthday breakfast, a table reserved – three young sisters.
They are politely quiet, almost whispering.
When the eldest rises to leave for work –
a kiss on the forehead for her kin.

I imagine my three sisters rescued.

III.

The owner of Life Buoy, Jane,
who always gives a smile, and sometimes says hello,
brings to me a black-and-white portrait of a man –
suit and bow tie – from another era.

He looks just like me.

'Would you like this?', Jane says.

From the birthday table –
different people; different day –
an elderly lady agrees:

'Yes, that's what I thought
when I saw him earlier.
He looks like you.'

I don't know the man who looks like me.

I accept the painting.

IV.

Each Saturday morning I drink coffee,
edit poems for *The Walnut Tree*,
imagine the world can be rescued.

UNTITLED

For my mother, Veronica Wiggins.

    The

        mother

            writes

                the

            baby

    poem

A YORTA YORTA MAN

In memory of Jimmy Little,
1 March, 1937 – 2 April, 2012.

Includes words from Jimmy Little's song, 'Yorta Yorta Man'.

I.

I was born   on the banks   of the Murray...

      My totem is the long-necked turtle...

Yorta Yorta   is my mother's   tribal stand...

      This song is for my parents, and for my country...

I'm her son   but my father's name   I carry...

      From time to time, I write a new song...

As I walk   through this great   and ancient land...

      The river: it finds its way to me...

My spirit will go back one day   to my mother...

      I sing this song, with all my heart...

And to my father   like the boomerang.

II.

Today in the bush and in the city
we weep for you, Yorta Yorta Man.

A child listens to the sound of a sea shell,
centre-stage at the setting sun:

Yunupingu and Pigram and Archie and Sultan
and Anu and Mauboy and Donovan and Gurrumul...

Because of you, Yorta Yorta Man –
I will listen, and sing with my heart.

FACTORY AT RISDON COVE

A dying old man of the river –
with a shame in his heart; and a shiver.
A boy said: 'I won't wish you dead.'
Which saved that old man of the river.

A childhood (and mine), porky pies;
the weatherman forecast Derwent-blue skies;
the bream and the flathead were telling lies –
how peculiar the child if the river dies.

A mother above all, of temperance, hums;
the clerk of accounts, safeguards the sums.
Kids in the dust, crawl to their mums;
the boss in his Jaguar, jarosite runs.

Factory fords wake the cadmium ducks –
of Russian roulette these lead-laden trucks –
round-about – in-out – the toxic reflux
preening our skeleton smelter's black tux.

The boss in his Jaguar, jarosite runs;
kids in the dust, crawl to their mums.
The clerk of accounts, safeguards the sums;
a mother above all, of temperance, hums.

A childhood (and yours), porky pies;
the weatherman rostered-on Derwent-blue skies;
the gulls and the kites were telling lies –
how peculiar the child now the river dies.

A dying old man of the river –
with a shame in his heart; and a shiver.
A girl said: 'I won't wish you dead.'
Which saved that old man of the river.

A TERRA NULLIUS ELECTION

'We don't have any shelter but humanity.'

From an interview with Behrouz Boochani,
author of the book, *No Friend But The Mountains*.

Globe (warming & our canned oceans overflowing)...
Evangelical Prime Ministers' (green & gold) budgie-smugglers...
Tasmanian Devil (an island's comparatively small facial tumour)...
Kiss asylum seekers goodbye (*No Friend But The Mountains*)...
Eating secure borders (between Church & State)...
Fleets of the convict unemployed (rations of bread & water)...
Canoe foreign aid (one million human bones [not ours])...
Under a Boochani moon (the tide & aborigines of forty thousand years)...
The Australian (News Limited citizen of our watery globe)...

                sensing the old

                                      man's dementia

      loving word

                                              marvel

THE WRECKING YARD

each and every

                                                at the care

            to the chosen

                        listen

THE CLOCK-MAKER OF LAUNCESTON

After Benjamin Frater's book, *6am in the Universe*.

Clockwise –
9 am
in the universe...

Tick-tock,
tick-tock:
one-hundred clocks...

One grandfather clock,
two grandfather clocks,
three grandfather clocks...

The inner
workings of a
stilled clock...

SUN – clockwork
orange – the violence
of cogs and pulleys...

Wedding clock –
her friends drop hints
to Mr. Right...

Alarm! Adorable dog;
Hoosagood Boythen. Tick-tock:
pendulum-tailed clock...

The church clock
believes
it owns this town...

Your Dreamtime
in York Street –
EXPIRED...

Try this minute jimmy: gold
pocket watch
of my birth...

Henry For[war]d – *[b(l)ack]* –
turn the hand-crank:
putt-putt-*Vrrrroooooom!*...

Hurry!
Hurry!
Clockwise is MOVING...

Note:
John Clarke, 'Hoosagood Boythen'.

TIGER SNAKE

For the Gardner-Parker family.

I.

At her appointment with me
I assume the high ground...

The caravan is open
so that its eye is now

seeing south.
A haiku spills out...

The old caravan's
bent awning
did not just wink

II.

Just like a local
I offer directions

to the tiger snake –
'Mum's old Singer

sewing machine!'
The snake's jaw

into a canvas bag
before I can blink.

III.

A Falcon –
motoring the snake

along the winding
road to nowhere...

The promise
of a forest.

Note:
Haiku by Jeffrey Harpeng.

A BODY'S CIVIL WAR

In my home
I fall – a tripwire
invented by me –
my left femur broken
to smithereens, where
it ought to connect to the hip.

Four weeks I lay in the bunker
of the Launceston General...

I stand to the white flag
of a doctor... **Diagnosis:**
*AUTO-IMMUNE & ASSOCIATED
DISORDERS* (a body's civil war):

osteoporosis (one brittle soldier);
type 1 diabetes (insert a low G.I.
joke HERE) – *late onset;*
*anxiety; one blown inner-
ear* – this shell shall serve, as warning:
the eternal siren of *tinnitus* –
*meniere's syndrome – dizzy,
and no hearing to speak of
there now...* 'Remind me again,
which side is shot?'

*He lives
by a disability pension,
due* (not at all like reading in the dark
depression
of war, a letter from your waiting
lover) *to:*

chronic fatigue syndrome (synchronise watches) &
rheumatoid arthritis (stand-up straight, quick-march) &
(bullet) *powders, trigger-foods,* (the gun of)
perfumes (safe for humans) – *all falling under
multiple chemical hyper-sensitivity...*

I remember him saying something about that...

Auto-immune syndromes
(friendly-fire, the enemy)...

'Mmmmm...' *wiggles nose*

Could it be this man is not a hypochondriac?

In future wars
I hope for a doctor
who is less rifle-straight
when I make the merest
movement in the daylight,
or should I whisper
of the battleground...

A body's civil war –
my young life.

CRICKET IS PROOF OF ETERNITY

'Happiness and team spirit comes from within.'

Sir Donald Bradman, *Farewell to Cricket.*

Cricket is proof of eternity.
Every saint in the land loves Sir Don –
we lose not a wink over Bodyline;
we serve jam and cream with our scone.

> Cricket is proof of eternity.
> The dictionary defines the dead
> to be – *without life*. Here the living
> lie down to watch cricket in bed.

Cricket is proof of eternity.
Every saint in the land loves Sir Don –
we lose not a wink over Bodyline;
we serve jam and cream with our scone.

> Cricket is proof of eternity.
> In the grandstand the folk are bereft,
> for the preachers of Heaven on earth
> don't know the long days we have left...

Cricket is proof of eternity.
Every saint in the land loves Sir Don –
we lose not a wink over Bodyline;
we serve jam and cream with our scone.

> Cricket is proof of eternity.
> The lost, the downtrodden, the lame,
> wander the streets with one question –
> is cricket any more than a game?

Cricket is proof of eternity.
Every saint in the land loves Sir Don –
we lose not a wink over Bodyline;
we serve jam and cream with our scone.

> Cricket is proof of eternity.
> A lost soul at the boundary fence;
> the 12th man, fated to the outer –
> never picked: now, then, nor hence.

Cricket is proof of eternity.
Every saint in the land loves Sir Don –
we lose not a wink over Bodyline;
we serve jam and cream with our scone.

> Cricket is proof of eternity.
> Pray, what will the man upstairs say?
> And what will he list as the reasons
> for sending this player on his way?

Cricket is proof of eternity.
Every saint in the land loves Sir Don –
we lose not a wink over Bodyline;
we serve jam and cream with our scone.

> Cricket is proof of eternity.
> 'Tis written on gold leaf, with quills –
> a young man bookmarks a page
> at the fading of light in the hills.

Cricket is proof of eternity.
Every saint in the land loves Sir Don –
we lose not a wink over Bodyline;
we serve jam and cream with our scone...

THE MEMORY OF A CYCLONE

Fannie Bay, Darwin – 2000.

Sunrise: Paul and Isabelle's Datsun, mould
spores fragrant; orange body torn from cold
Tasmanian pockets, creamy sponge cake
fingers, and icy flits out to Great Lake...

Chemist man: on the way out. Pretty surf
girl, under glass Hangin' Ten at the birth
of Cyclone Tracy. The dark-skied cell, locked;
history as hangman; a life-force, hocked...

Sunrise: *throb* and the long-grassers begin;
crocodile cliffs yawn; serpents take a swim;
Paul (and co-pilot), horizontal; dogs'
bones, song and songlines, dropped dead at the jog.

A BIT OF HEALTHY CONVERSATION

I.

Cross
the
desert...

Three road trains
travelling shot gun
to outsmart the pigs.

Country pub –
the melancholy purse
of an old man's lips.

Monday – the sound
of a whip bird but no
school bell.

We are making
a flog
of money.

II.

The Apple Isle's
fruit and vegetable man
talks to his customers

as if in a patch
of peas and corn –
quietly...

Like a psychiatrist,
but with healthier
props.

THE ENCYCLOPEDIAS OF VAN DIEMEN'S LAND

For a child:
the world

of facts
at the supermarket.

Mother:
the free

in-house
promotion.

Stubbing-out
the facts:

'How many
does it take?'

One carton
of cigarettes:

one volume of facts,
encyclopedic.

Ants' print:
aardvark

to zyzzyva.
In the palm

of a mother's hand:
a boy

letting go the hand
of his education.

Flame:
cathedral cigarette;

ecclesiastic
lip lines.

Love,
filtered

Fortune: a drag
to the last gasp.

Life is a
cigarette:

in Hobart's empty-packet times.
A mother:

will never be far
from such a cause.

Just one last
Vandemonian lag:

from the day
the child quits.

VAN DIEMEN'S LAND

The spray
in question:

water displacer,
WD-40. Works

on my treasure like quick-
silver. All of the

answers are taken:
an island's

dead head
frontal lobe –

X-marks-the-spot –
stolen.

Transportation's mechanic
in question: 'Which donk

tool would you choose
if not this spanner-in-a-can?

We are shipwrecked
on Van Diemen's Land.'

FOG

Commonly known as the Bridgewater Jerry, a fog infiltrates along the Derwent River in Hobart...

Bridgewater Jerry, floats on her belly...

I needed some gold coins
a few moons

ago at the laundrette —
Cold-Cold:

I walk to the OASIS,
I ask for ten.

A paper cup
of coins —

the barmaid smiles:
'Sure, Love —

good luck!'
I exit the Oasis.

Egret and I
fly home from regret.

Moons
ago at the laundrette.

Bridgewater Jerry, floats on her belly...

THE JOCKEY-WHEEL OF FAITH

For Sir Isaac and Mr King.

Man finds his purpose and his fix:
a jockey-wheel and a six-foot-tall crucifix.

Of Earthly transit, and branching zeal,
the crucifix rolls on a rubber wheel.

This old man of the white-sneakered test –
long white socks, high-viz vest.

At BWS, where the faithful buy grog,
a pamphlet is proffered to a *lost soul* and his dog.

To wait in Earth's queue – 'Please, Mate – don't ask.'
Hard-working hands are made just for the task,

so he'll roll-in Scottsdale's New Year. Crucifix and frown,
a lonely street preacher in a country town.

ENDEAVOUR AT THE OPERA HOUSE

South Hobart.

For Ben Guy.

After Molly Guy's 'More Lost Sock Laundrette'.

James cooks in a convict kitchenette
the size of a bathtub. The bathtub itself
his convict mates can see through the mist of green tea.
A plate of buttered islands away

Endeavour rests beneath the Huon pine stairs –
this poor prosthetic, passed down
the family line to the first-born.

Endeavour wears a tall white
walking sock and an old leather boot.

Next door, Hobart's The Salad Bowl
caters for hollow legs.

In black-and-white photos, James'
various hobnailed poses –
snapped at our city's icy
intersections – traffic lights dazzle and blur –
the effect of granting a wish to the place
where a thigh bone, once upon a time
connected to the hip bone –
a chorus line, stolen at midnight.

At the *dawn of time*,
James sings from the bathtub
across to the cast-aside oyster shells
(a modern midden):
the Sydney Opera House.

James' operatic voice
soars to the loft's sleeping chambers,
rattling convict bricks
and chains...

In the moonlight,
when James is told of *Endeavour's*
pedestrian truth: he was not alone
while he sang – James cries,

'But I sang an operetta!'

MERMAID

In memory of Aunt Rene, who lived house-bound due to rheumatoid arthritis.

After an ABC radio interview with a professional mermaid.

hello
      I'm a mermaid widow

            it's not my creation   no
                  she's from a moonbeam

      or the dying Great Barrier Reef

   I can't take the credit for it
       for me it was always
            a long journey to safe water
       now I live
    just five minutes to the beach
I get to swim like a mermaid
      today see my tail-fin
          kick butt
              to the bottom of the pool...

        there are many aspects to being
     a mermaid
we each have our own issues

     disempowering?   no
        once I am in the water
           who is going to catch me?

					since I got my licence
			I see a lot of mermaids
	what about you?
				a fantasy life
						or dual realities
									you can be happy
												living in two worlds

												my tail-fin has tiny little scales
							sprinkled all over it
	& I have some silicone (from Bunnings)
holding me together

DETOURS

Campbell Town, Tasmania.

'Bring one good face into this house today.'
You Am I (Tim Rogers), 'Hourly Daily'.

Of dirt music –
and at Banjos

a string of
slowly rising

council workers
lay rock

cakes
upon lovely

tongues –
encore!

Notes:
Tim Winton, *Dirt Music*.

A WISDOM OF WOMBATS

For the Spencer / Nolan family and Margaret Mountney (Taylor).
'Wisdom' is the collective noun for a group of wombats.

The first night,
I shine a light

upon the tired marsupial
wallpaper in my tin-miner's cottage.

An Australiana print,
one I would later learn

to be of the family's indelible
patterns. There is much to discover

and to be distracted by
as I imagine mining the past –

a wombat
under the house, for example.

When death is dug by history so keen,
a wisdom that you might never have been.

HOW TO READ A POEM

*After Les Murray's poetry reading at Sydney University,
August 20, 2015 – YouTube.*

You are here to read from *Waiting for the Past*.
Your black baseball cap shadows the organ.
The future is a time beyond denim.
Shuffle feet and inches

for the timbre of a lectern.
Lift the loose arms of your reading
glasses, half-moons, a universal
miracle your book

must have been there all along.
Baseball cap *off*. Les Murray
return to your age. Grin.
Maybe it's getting a bit worn

it wants a rest the new book.
How about some old poems? Let's try 1976.
And so I've stuck all these bits of paper
in here – lick a finger, turn the page, breathe…

We can hear you
breathing just like you
do it at Bunyah.
Don't read everything

you have planned, read silently
to the audience rummage until you find…
I used to write too long;
so now I write too short – ha!

A poem you fancy. Two handfuls
of languages lips: a tongue
like this one is rare –
nothing is free when it is explained.

You are approaching eighty,
your right hand holds the book,
shakes forever the BIG
machinery of your crane poem,

a stanza from which you tell us
is pinned to the dash of Sweeney's
crane, he likes it so much –
CLUNK – this microphone doesn't like me:

These machines are inclined
to maintain a beast like world war,
in which we turn over everything,
to provide unceasing victories.

Arrive at the end,
check your wristless watch –
ah, the timing is right
for the last poem.

End with a cliff-hanger...
Or an aeroplane poem –
not from The Biplane Houses,
this one flies out from London Sexburga Airport...

Belly-laugh, watch us
do the same, though for us
our belly isn't as hungry.
We wish we were.

Reach without pause
your shadow for the hidden
goblet of red wine,
ready for questions.

Don't look down your nose
unless it is for your first sip...
Or did you have a sip earlier?
Answers. Baseball cap *on:*

YouTube will never know...

AUDEN'S WEB

Last night I squashed a funnel web spider
with Auden's *As I Walked Out One Evening –
songs, ballads, lullabies, limericks and
other light verse...*

Note:
W.H. Auden, *As I Walked Out One Evening – songs,
ballads, lullabies, limericks and other light verse.*

PENNY-FARTHING

A penny-farthing for your dreams:
along Lullaby Road skyscraper spokes spin...

Upon a sleepy cloud, the stars
as your mother's love, you are

awoken one last time
by the silver bird bell: now

tuck-in your chin, Lullaby Road
shall deliver you to sleep...

Trace ten wishes, round
and round and round and round...

Sleep is for the brave
and true of heart.

Lullaby Road –
you know this like the cradled

palms of your present
penny-farthing hands...

BLUE DERBY

For Baba (Malcolm) Taylor.

In Tasmania's temperate north-east, a road worships monolith bales
and a mountain of stone, on the way to the world's great trails.

A zephyr caresses, as you quiet yourself for the dream
of those mountain bike trails of Derbyshire, where the riders flow like the stream...

At Derbyshire Manor – *melythina tiakana warrana* – the heart;
where a peaceful sleep will be yours tonight, by day the mountain bikes dart.

To the myth: a giant rainbow trout sleeps... Families of platypus quiver
at the morning mist of your thoughts along the Ringarooma River.

Eat the mountain for breakfast! Pancakes, honey and cream.
Pour a hot coffee... Ponder the sound of a black currawong's keen.

For the guests, dry-stone walls are a temple, built by father and son. Look
in wonder through any window you choose. Walk these steps, an open book...

There are roses, fox gloves, fuchsias and lupins – for day-lily eyes, rubbed open;
the fruit trees are plump with peaches and plums – the flesh of morning, awoken.

What do you hear? That's called *silence*. Of the stringy-barks, it won't be long
'till you're pedalling past the ghost of a bullocky, to the earth-beat of the mountain bikes' song.

Climb-up; rouse the early morning straggler; set your wheel to the cobble-stones, neat:
a sprint, or one long, yawning wheel-stand, along Derbyshire's main street.

This is the *Trail of the Tin Dragon*, where our Chinese townsfolk of tin
rode horse-and-cart – as if beside you now – neighbour, and kin.

Back when each day dragged a lengthened chain – the time between dawn and dusk, wide –
Derbyshire, a wild wheel of pubs... Today, a map of trails you'll ride...

And when your crank-it heart is full, at the end of the day on these trails,
perhaps you'll adjourn for a brew – or two – and hear from the locals the tales

of life in the north-east, at Derbyshire, in the town where our old-timers know –
life is a precious, fertile land: *You reap what you sow...*

For a trip to this town is a nourishment, and a trail to a life that is new,
though set in the old ways, of the humble. Who knows, the trail may find *you*.

Now is your moment to shine. So let your worries fly away with the hawk.
In the forest of your mind, sit high above the mountain bike fork...

In perfect flow, kiss your loved ones; take your mountain bike to the sky...
Two roads diverged in a wood, and I – I took the one less travelled by.

Notes:
melythina tiakana warrana means: heart of country,
Aboriginal language, north-eastern Tasmania.
Robert Frost, 'The Road Not Taken', 1916.

POSTIE

For the folk of Pioneer, Tasmania.

In my home town of Pioneer, everyone rides a postie bike.
What could be more natural? To post one's personality like...

Sally's has a wicker basket, carrying local history and honey;
chain-smoking is the red Suzuki revved by Rhino Johnny.

Nancy, quiet as a church mouse, yearly posts us each a note;
Bazza, the rough-voiced Russian, grants us gemstones from his coat.

Jen's steed, four-legged, is an exception to the rule;
the Mayor and GM, on a tandem bike, stubborn as a mule.

Megan, savior of cats and dogs: in a side-cart she is chauffeured
with her sister, Tanya. Wallabies hitch a ride without a word.

Trevor gives a grin: wit is seldom delivered too often;
Sean's postie bike's macabre: trailing behind it is a coffin.

Paula has The Dolls' House now – her postie bike is tiny;
from Joseph Lyons' street, Tim posts poems, new and shiny.

In the town of Pioneer, everyone rides a postie bike...
Why can't we all pretend to post the Royal Mail like...

A LOTUS OF LAWYERS
Cradle to the Grave

For the men, women and children of Pioneer, Tasmania, the long journey to secure safe drinking water, following a recurring risk from heavy metals.

*The lotus flower is traditionally associated with purity and rebirth – it blooms daily, retracts to the mud at night, flowering clean the following day.
Lotus is a brand of sports car, known for its convertible skin.*

    A Lotus of lawyers
        A caesarian of lawyers

    A lullaby of lawyers
        A little let-off of lawyers

    A rattle of lawyers
        A pram and *walk-free* of lawyers

    A slippery-slide of lawyers
        A see-saw of lawyers

    A princess lawyer
        A cowboy lawyer

    A lasso of lawyers
        A loophole of lawyers

    A law school of lawyers
        A school yard *Fight! Fight! Fight!* of lawyers

    The principal lawyer...
        A graduation of lawyers!

    A spin-the-bottle of lawyers...
        The first kiss of lawyers (dare)

A prima facie of lawyers
        A poker facey of lawyers

A courting of lawyers
        A screwing of lawyers

The white *w[h]ine* of lawyers
        A lazy Susan of lawyers

A live lobster of lawyers
        A lockdown of lawyers

A lobotomy of lawyers
        A living will of lawyers

A plot of lawyers
        A graveyard of lawyers

A lie of lawyers
        A Lotus of lawyers…

SKEET, THE WOODMAN

In memory of Brian (Skeet) and Carol McCarthy.

Everyone loves Skeet, the woodman.
At last count, seventy-three, Skeet collects antique
chainsaws. He flashes his forever-broad and toothy
smile beneath a bird's nest of curls.

Skeet's tilt-tray truck returns...
On a good day (every day is a good day),
Skeet talks four tons of firewood into falling
one inchman ant's length from a woodshed.

Skeet's nickname comes from the contraption that catapults
for a shooter's aim. So at the pub when the town calls: *'PULL!'* –
Skeet throws another log to the fire,
and cold beer flows like a river...

Skeet has had more beers, more splinters –
more than Winnaleah has ever had winters.
Skeet has known more sunrises, more calls of *'Timmm-beerrrrrr!'* –
more than the Ringarooma River can remember.

Four seasons in one day: Skeet's unassuming
voice possesses an endearing way of holding the word
'like' to every heartfelt phrase. Skeet said,
'That'll be a good little heater for you like.'

These were Skeet's words of kindling kindness
for my first *chimley* winter here at Pioneer,
as he gently released from his embrace
a new wood heater to rest upon the hearth.

As I write, with a cosy fire crackling,
thinking of Skeet, and his dear wife, Carol –
I imagine these towns, with their humble cottages, cold
if not for the warmth from the honest within our fold.

THE GUM LEAF PLAYER

I.   *Finding Belief (the leaf)*

Spanning a forest of years
at last I have stumbled upon
how to find a good one:

I can pick a gum leaf wearing a blindfold.

I don't hold belief playing any other leaf –
lips and tongue, I've tried them all,
but nothing musical seems to come

out of them – *squeak, squeak!*

To play the gum leaf, to hold
a tune, neatly fold in two;
like a koala, I breathe and chew

in concert. A holiday from the gum trees,

I play in a five-piece
gum leaf band. We played John
and Yoko's *Imagine* to re-open

Sydney Harbour Bridge...

II.   *Finding Love (true love)*

I met my wife at a discotheque...
Also a contraption to catapult, to hook clay birds into the air...
The Salvation Army, one with a trumpet...
You beside the dance floor, what do you cry for? Let's live it up...
The prize was a brand new suit of sails...
Dance as breath – a full moon – breath as dance...
Kiss: 'I can pick a gum leaf wearing a blindfold'...

Notes:
John Lennon and Yoko Ono, 'Imagine'.
Mental as Anything, 'Live It Up'.

UNREASONABLE HAPPINESS

For Esther Ottaway.

Includes happiness prevailing over unsupportive circumstances and / or
the expectations of an individual or a society... Plus a potential association
relating to happiness as a quality available to women, sometimes
in opposition to the assumptions and / or the placation of men and their belief
in the ownership of reason and women... Plus happiness as the unexpected:
a surprise... Plus happiness as a planned destination, listening to the heart
above all else... Plus for you, faith as a source of happiness... Plus happiness
cannot be reasoned... Plus a possible evocation of the senses... Plus a challenge to
the definition of happiness...

CHILD AND GRANDFATHER

For Grant and his grandfather.

Includes lines from David Malouf's poem, 'Before or After'.

In his old age
the great poet writes:
It is the small

*the muted inconsequential,
at this point that comes closest
to real.*

In the sunshine of this
autumn morning, the car park is empty –
except for these fallen leaves...

A child stands still at the centre;
his grandfather quietly
brings for the boy a broom.

The broom is taller than the boy,
bristle-head is broader than the child is tall.
His grandfather steps away...

Shining
the boy's fine hair
sweeps his forehead from sleep.

The boy takes one giant step,
finds one perfect push: the broom
sweeps golden leaves...

The smiling child –
he and his grandfather –
together, in balance...

I smile: I thought I knew this boy.
As though his first steps this year
his only concentration. But no –

the child. His grandfather looks to me –
for one moment – smiles, blushes
at the witness of his fortune

and this humble teaching.
The great poet ends his poem:
Dustmotes

in a sunshaft ascendant.
Before or after
the fact.

THE FUTURE LIBRARY

Pioneer, Tasmania – 2013.

(a bookcase falls upon a young poet)

The heavenly
book.

Falling.
The tree

of books.
Falling.

Leaves
fall.

Falling
I am

a leaf.
Fallen

I lie –
of books

& the flat-Earth
bookmark.

THE ANT

'What has no shadow has no strength to live.'
From Czeslaw Milosz's poem, 'The World'.

The ant travels
along his cosmic line,
casting a tiny shadow –

bravely,
upon the blank page
of a poet.

The typewriter
as our planet:
return, return, return...

Other ants join in
as one – hope is
a lexicon –

tickles
cuticles
for a poem...

Acknowledgements

All reasonable attempts have been made to contact copyright owners. The author wishes to thank the following copyright owners: Tim Winton, Jim Everett – puralia meenamatta, Jonathon Kimberley, Frances Peters-Little for Jimmy Little, Tim Rogers / You Am I (Universal Music), G. Macainsh (Skyhooks, Mushroom Records), Andy Jackson, Behrouz Boochani, W.H. Auden, Nicole Frater for Benjamin Frater, John Clarke, Clive James, Czeslaw Milosz, David Malouf, Sir Donald Bradman, George Mackay Brown, Jeffrey Harpeng, John Lennon / Yoko Ono, Les Murray, Margaret Scott, Andrew 'Greedy' Smith, Rachael Guy for Molly Guy, Robert Frost and Sarah Day.

The following poems have been published previously, some in earlier versions.

'Thylacine': Commissioned by John Brakey of Weldborough Hotel, Weldborough, Tasmania, 2021.

'The Green Religion': *The Weekend Australian*, Jaya Savige, 2019.

'The Wand of the Sea' (previously 'Dementia-Deep'): *Australian Poetry Anthology*, Volume 8, Melinda Smith and Sara Saleh, 2020.

'The Funeral': *Grieve,* Ross Gillett and Judy Johnson, 2017.

'Teacup of the Rose': Margaret Reid International Poetry Prize, Honourable Mention, Soma Mei Sheng Frazier, 2019.

'A Yorta Yorta Man': *The Koori Mail*, Kirstie Parker, 2015.

'A Terra Nullius Election' (previously 'An Australian Election'): *Tasmanian Times*, Lindsay Tuffin, 2015.

'A Body's Civil War': *Growing Up Disabled In Australia*, Carly Findlay, Black Inc., 2021.

'Blue Derby' (previously 'On the Road to Derbyshire Manor'): Commissioned by Daniel Taylor of Derbyshire Manor, Derby, Tasmania, 2018.

'A Lotus of Lawyers': *Cordite Poetry Review*, Nathan Curnow, 2019.

'Skeet, the Woodman': Displayed by Virginnia Wells at Federal Tavern, Derby, Tasmania, 2019.

Thank you

I respect this land of lutruwita / Tasmania. I Acknowledge the Aboriginal people of this land, which was never ceded. I recognise their continuing connection to land, water and community. I pay respect to Elders past, present and emerging.

For their mentorship, generosity and friendship, thank you: Esther Ottaway, Daniela Brozek Cordier, Sarah Day, Jim Everett - puralia meenamatta, Karen Knight, Andy Jackson, Tom Joyce, Jaya Savige, Molly Guy, Rachael Guy, Pete Hay, Colin Berry, Louise Oxley, Cameron Hindrum and David Mason. Thanks to Robert McDonald for his stunning painting, the cover for this book.

For her belief in me, thank you to my sister, Ebony Slade. Thanks to the loyal friends and family who have contributed to the writing of this book in so many different ways, with special mention to Lisa Rime and my niece, Danah Slade. Thank you to the wonderful teachers who have enriched my life. Cheers to John Brakey of Weldborough Hotel, and to my friends, new and old. In memory of Brett Skipper and Shane Joseph. For sharing your love and patience with me, thank you to my family – Wiggins, Slade, Lehman, Lovell, McDonald, Saltmarsh, and beyond. Perpetual pats to Lolly the cat, my loyal and ever-present reader...

Thank you to all who have read *The Walnut Tree*.
This book is the last known trace of the tree's life.

www.ingramcontent.com/pod-product-compliance
Lightning Source LLC
Chambersburg PA
CBHW020329010526
44107CB00054B/2046